CELEBRATING THE CITY OF BUCHAREST

Celebrating the City of Bucharest

Walter the Educator

Silent King Books
A WhichHead Entertainment Imprint

Copyright © 2024 by Walter the Educator

All rights reserved. No part of this book may be reproduced in any manner whatsoever without written per- mission except in the case of brief quotations embodied in critical articles and reviews.

First Printing, 2024

Disclaimer

This book is a literary work; the story is not about specific persons, locations, situations, and/or circumstances unless mentioned in a historical context. Any resemblance to real persons, locations, situations, and/or circumstances is coincidental. This book is for entertainment and informational purposes only. The author and publisher offer this information without warranties expressed or implied. No matter the grounds, neither the author nor the publisher will be accountable for any losses, injuries, or other damages caused by the reader's use of this book. The use of this book acknowledges an understanding and acceptance of this disclaimer.

Celebrating the City of Bucharest is a little collectible souvenir book that belongs to the Celebrating Cities Book Series by Walter the Educator. Collect them all and more books at WaltertheEducator.com

USE THE EXTRA SPACE TO TAKE NOTES AND DOCUMENT YOUR MEMORIES

BUCHAREST

In the heart of Romania, where whispers of history entwine,

Celebrating the City of Bucharest

Lies Bucharest, a city where past and present align.

From the cobblestones of Lipscani, stories ancient and grand,

To the modern pulse of Unirii, where today's footsteps stand.

The Dâmbovița flows, a ribbon of shimmering light,

Through parks where the linden trees offer respite.

The Palace of the Parliament, a colossal giant so grand,

Whispers of Ceaușescu's dreams, carved by iron hand.

Archways of Macca-Vilacrosse, a blend of old and new,

In cafes, the laughter of youth, in every shadow, a view.

Caru' cu Bere, where time's embrace lingers sweet,

Celebrating the City of Bucharest

Echoes of revelry, where heartbeats and rhythms meet.

Autumn's gold embraces Herăstrău's expansive embrace,

While in spring, Cişmigiu blooms with a gentle grace.

Each boulevard tells tales of revolutions and change,

Of a city reborn, in a cadence both wild and strange.

The Athenaeum stands, domed in majestic grace,

Echoing melodies that time cannot erase.

The old and the new dance a waltz in the street,

Where history and progress effortlessly meet.

In markets, the vibrant pulse of life thrums clear,

Peasant blouses, fresh fruits, the buzz of the here.

Piața Obor, where aromas and colors collide,

A mosaic of culture, in Bucharest's pride.

Churches with frescoes, where faith's whispers reside,

Patriarchal reflections, where shadows confide.
Celebrating the City of
Bucharest

Stavropoleos, where silence is a hymn so profound,

Within the Byzantine beauty, sanctity found.

Bucharest by night, a tapestry of light and sound,

In clubs and bars, where beats and laughter resound.

The city never sleeps, its heart ever awake,

In the vibrant nightlife, new dreams take shape.

The people, resilient, with a spirit unbowed,

From struggles and triumphs, their voices loud.

Faces tell stories, of a land rich and deep,

Of hopes and aspirations they ardently keep.

Celebrating the City of
Bucharest

Beneath the skyline, where contrasts play,

Bucharest is a symphony, in a perpetual sway.

Old world charm and new age flair,

A city of contrasts, a jewel rare.

ABOUT THE CREATOR

Walter the Educator is one of the pseudonyms for Walter Anderson. Formally educated in Chemistry, Business, and Education, he is an educator, an author, a diverse entrepreneur, and he is the son of a disabled war veteran. "Walter the Educator" shares his time between educating and creating. He holds interests and owns several creative projects that entertain, enlighten, enhance, and educate, hoping to inspire and motivate you. Follow, find new works, and stay up to date with Walter the Educator™ at WaltertheEducator.com

www.ingramcontent.com/pod-product-compliance
Lightning Source LLC
LaVergne TN
LVHW012050070526
838201LV00082B/3895